IVH

IV H

An Alphamath Serial

Victor Coleman

BookThug
2012

FIRST EDITION

The production of this book was made possible through the generous assistance of The Canada Council for The Arts and The Ontario Arts Council.

Canada Council for the Arts Conseil des Arts du Canada

ONTARIO ARTS COUNCIL
CONSEIL DES ARTS DE L'ONTARIO

The author thanks the Toronto Arts Council for time to write.

TORONTO ARTS COUNCIL

Thanks to Michael Boughn and David Peter Clark for critiques and response.

LIBRARY AND ARCHIVES CANADA
CATALOGUING IN PUBLICATION

Coleman, Victor, 1944-
ivH : an alphamath serial / Victor Coleman.

Poems.
Also issued in electronic format.
ISBN 978-1-927040-36-2

I. Title.

PS8505.O455I95 2012 C811'.54 C2012-905405-4

PRINTED IN CANADA

l'Histoire avec sa grande hache

– Georges Perec, *W ou le souvenir d'enfance*

*

"No victor believes in chance."

– Nietzsche

IVH one

Stopped on the edge
with eyes in balls
the procession
galloped along
shouting "Open!"
The balconies
of languages
appeared in clouds.

The occupants'
necks tightened in
the final stage,
they carried a
yellow object,
a parasol,
with ellipsoids
in the windows.

An iron plate
equipped with skin,
two long wood slats
striking one long
decorated
contortionist,
eyes figuring
one hundred flags.

Autocthones with
some exceptions
taken hostage
could not make that
population
remarkable –
the major part
because it worked.

The British Base
with the eyes of
young children so
natural in
uniform, large
and fair, presents
nurses, women,
persons on leave.

The Chinese like
their yellow fall,
not so funny
to form so much,
since all soldiers
arrive on time
because their knives
held no more joy.

A circle round
which no mimes rent
whose place was bound –
the gravity
elected them –
they laugh, they laugh
because they do
not understand.

One could say cats
with violins
and instruments
of other tones
sing to reflect
the air of Kings
with one who draws
what they like best.

IVH two

Chinese advance
was preceded
by open valves –
two policemen
with soughs in eyes
left galloping –
many merchants
in procession.

A tram went up
the Asian file,
with tightened necks,
shouting windows
in curious
high balconies
of coagu-
lation's last stage.

Barbarians
showed me their short
silence to work
its contempt for
the Emperor –
my mother chose
another tone
to amplify.

Thinking famous,
speech looked finished –
the bottom of
his hateful thoughts –
a combustion
however hot,
always too much
human being.

Sunday chickens
who feared the herds
can't need to know
new Emperors
who're born to hope.
Stories scoff in
estimation,
duck them often.

We went slowly
because of our
legitimate
solitary
office transport,
which followed cause
funicular
while sucking air.

Not famous – good,
fateful – fifteen
years of service:
Here is my friend
a little drawn.
Civil servants
said it was great
to find more joy.

In spite of their
forecast, charming
idiots may
not need truth, a
combustion of
contempt – simply
amplify news –
which thought requires.

IVH three

Dandelions
allowed him to
escape from thirst
with blows and more
guns which ends
very vulgar
inaccurate prose
with family.

His father died
tragically –
one wife who would
descend in the
middle of her
thought was widowed –
his mother's love
was my true faith.

Our childhood was
memory, sounds
of bad gasses –
dream appliquéd
its youth also –
civil servants
who believe in
solid masses.

The Chinese days
were found in front
ruminating
in the city
until terminals
came to hear the
population
transmit phonemes.

Acoustics of
artillery
only journalists
explain, transmit
ignorance down,
looked at the hour
concludes its pipes
conceal return.

The small girl then
in fourteen years
paid imprudence
following the
stamp on the front.
Inflated trams
examined more
quiet moments.

Customs remained
towards a large
city judged good,
its eyes more blue
than very young,
purely redden
prey for the flag
a satyr's kiss.

Canadian
girls have small skirts –
centres made with
funny pockets –
on the platform
she's very young
who cannot speak
the end of time.

IVH four

Asylum of
short-sighted eyes
flickered obscure –
culture error,
books arrayed and
dirty candy –
one slight shop in
the gas lit street.

Non-existent
intelligence
did not have gas
in times of peace –
the province of
old amateurs
disposed to rare
old salt libraries.

Never had the
mildewed taste of
native clients
provided peace.
Sparse capital
even with war
holding upright
with the modern.

Even daily
publications
were satisfied
in addition –
some delighted –
one tube was to
blunt the thing it
could not accept.

A very weak
opening could
not encompass
release – its coarse
loathing of less
as much because
some hated it
in the corner.

While reading God
he lived alone –
bent, washed, swept, cooked –
widowed even –
purchaser of
naked silver
initially
his idea.

Badly used for
firing its taste,
the good city
did not abound –
had recently
made, with the gleam
of spirit, some
beautiful books.

However, some
distant spirit,
accustomed to
philosophy,
knows moreover
one grave involved
in the mix of
released darkness.

IVH five

Not to suffer
small histories
or take my place
with what had fun –
to roast my too
expensive air,
assiduous,
however known.

A hundred times
misery would
gain small moves dealt
forward, needing
to never be
wrongly avenged
for his former faith
in my dry light.

I say people
who hear middle
class example,
stupid rabble,
under a room
of, blood work pre-
text – injustice
of freemasons.

I do not pay
my rent, ashamed –
his officers,
too disgusted,
continued true
work in justice –
it would like to
rain in my room.

This poor old man
who sold his book
the other day,
obliged to fire
undiscovered
high-school pupil,
continued still
one hundred weeks.

Middle-class proles
without a chance
do not play with
anything poor –
one hundred boards –
pennies ashamed
to be denied
Virgin parents.

I do not have
the specimen
Voltaire wanted.
I wrote to him
every week.
The other day
a forward fish
set up some noise.

Businessman
took his address,
would have done much
with a marine,
sailor surprised.
He told me life
was a naval
conversation.

IVH six

It is known as
a filthy book
but not great fish.
The innocent
wrongfully con-
demned, beautiful
man raised Voltaire
to one's defense.

Silent lament
failed to pronounce
squeaking of teeth,
business noise.
Oppressed parents
set up shoulders,
but no such chance
was on the boat.

How that be fact
I do not know.
His family's
conversation
with a sailor
about his boat,
said there's going
to be a war.

If you speak to
five unhappy
Marines, include
two years of sur-
prised arrival
over there as
all officers
understand it.

I was going
to undermine
one address, his
very ashamed
remainder wrote –
bearing manners,
took notes about
his own horrors.

Campaign begins,
would perhaps be
famous, become
terrible press –
one could not pay
more attention –
was not perchance
of my poor town.

Barbarians
wanting to speak,
silent children
lost husbands and
presence perceived
as back-story
about the top-
icality.

Old Emperor
filled and enthused,
considering
you say he died
a poor old man,
"bloody old pork"
with public death.
You know this book?

IVH seven

Neighbours chatter –
not the current
private life of
mourning cities.
Impressions speak
thus to evoke
live savages
about to grow.

Dreaming of his
cutting laughter,
reading factors
imperial
books unknown – you're
wrong: science can't
recognize it's
approbation.

The first time my
son entered the
landscape, many
rooms were outside
all accounts, things
for profit went
to ground, gone, but
never shipwrecked.

Night disappeared
as it began,
in dream – not
known again – green
costumed figures,
streaming, hands me
an astonished,
frightening day.

Too many dreams
would have liked to
haunt their bridges.
Turns about, spoke
first arrival –
bastard misled
my husband who'd
already died.

To hear one come
and read in old
Switzerland turns
crumpled pages
into fifty
centimes per hour –
this edition
seems expensive.

The boulevard,
it is murmured,
goes away from
instead of up –
added neutral
need – perhaps not
gone too quickly
towards the street.

The Stock exchanged
its heavy oil
for white water
close to the wood.
A group of kids
crossed – snotty-nosed,
frank gangsters all –
abandoned face.

IVHeight

The route of each
meridian
succeeded now
towards the same
children waiting
close to the fort –
not to counter
one's own being.

Patiently he
appeared single,
waited one hour
fearing satyrs,
then discovered
regular walks
had brought the news.
They did not come.

A questionnaire
was organized
each fifteen days,
then ev'ry week,
methodical.
Rarely did their
predilection
turn communal.

The little boy,
more or less small,
drawing this part
of the city.
One fine day they
suddenly con-
front him, equal
in the same tram.

One girl was both,
her memory,
more or less, well
found, incarnate
intensity,
delicate fresh,
grace astonished
this transpierced flesh.

Son-in-law in
newfound darkness
illuminates
this insane flame
which could support
a child of night
to hardly meet
that small girl's smile.

Her brother said,
"Flash your pocket
watch." the other
day. Mister pushed
her little badge
without elbows.
Excavated
with conviction.

The little boy
who said your leak
was small is known
as turning tight
without looking
then finally errs
with a tone to
catch what you want.

IVH nine

The Regiment
was overcome
the other day
by the girl known
as Wound of War,
who said to me,
"Which doctors made
some solemn knot?"

Little boy made
an endpaper
to impress you,
letting us see
crown deposit,
South Staffordshire.
I will write it –
seeing is king.

Carefully drawn
the name came back
with all its turns
impressed your large
Comrades without
knowing all the
capitals on
this small girl's lute.

Children known as
premises speak
English all day –
exaggerate
perfect accent,
known to excel.
These two, so nice,
have many friends.

Girlfriend reddens,
always ready
to sell any
collection, give
beautiful things –
some even have
continued with
the badge you need.

Without wormhole
it isn't you,
but let us see:
my small fear not
known to denounce
anything you
killed – defended
traffic badges.

You cannot be
children of war,
all alone by
the streets of fear.
You have badly
wounded leg – they
were proud of him,
like you were there.

Yes, of course, with
fear of that voice
and where to go?
Lead them to the
Saint-Maglore school,
as the small girl
before the war
goes to college.

IVH 10

Went to college,
gone communal
before the war.
Many older
sisters pay us
chocolate, street
smarter, murmured
"*éclair*, of course."

I wanted to
tell you something:
Be wise, well known,
our school, over
there, my children
re-examined,
she stopped to say,
"Goodbye – work well".

Little boy says
I would like to
see beautiful
true collections,
unknown badges
forcing laughter.
Let us see for
just one Sunday.

Come next Sunday
after the month's
end Cinema,
Wise Owl will ask
the lost little
boy, "You know my
name?" Imagine
that if you can.

You do not have
your name and your
present address
given on an
envelope which
showed him I, not
the regiment,
had penmanship.

Name the small boy,
the English one
that was not asked
to move away.
Expressed further
it looked to them
like some small girl
called to await.

Come *route précis*
meridian.
Advertising
returns towards
running brother –
says I am him.
Annette called one
who's joining her.

That first day's hour
won't counter them,
as they appear
close to the fort.
Succeeded there
and led each day
a single walk
towards being.

IVH 11

The Senator
did not believe
in going to
lunch after each
Sunday mass
with his brother
either to praise
guns or butter.

Visits quickly,
some minutes
constitute the
courtesy front –
some considered
religion good
to populate
a Sunday church.

One never saw
the omega
and alpha of
deranged practice –
devotion to
her brother for
these memories
once secular.

Uncertainty
evaporates,
succeeding in
making a share
of radical
military
opinions with
younger persons.

Acting without
resistance had
this old husband
beginning to
deliver some
authorized war
tolerated
by the clergy.

Protection of
our brave hairy
men over there
advised even
the Catholics
in sight of the
special uses
under the shells.

Her son-in-law
the *nationale*
was granted his
exemption from
exceptional
union title
because the priests
had gone to fight.

Unions like these
held exits close,
to parse the good
and the upright
church finally
made belief with
the good in the
other's evil.

IVH 12

Quickly it slipped
at once with speed
not wanting to
hear them beseech
churchgoers' sky
after coffee –
the safety of
third republics.

Senator Storm,
of the city
Navy station,
had crowned one when
water arrived
for her brothers:
dehorned cuckolds
on midday blow.

The Bosches can't see
nor will they like
other winters –
arranged shelters
were excellent –
news of which Charles
said, without coal
the pigs will freeze.

You think there are
foot warmers in
the trenches here?
Perfectly thus
ends perfectly.
I am not known
as simply truth
nor pessimist.

When the truth is
black it is known
as Senator
and does not count;
when it is white,
for example,
truth is very
beautiful now.

My sister was
bursting with real
hunger, she said
"Hold that table!"
Do you not find
that beautiful?
Therefore today
I open my mouth.

Thursday: movement,
the butter is
out of work, which
sends me more cakes.
Friday: make fun
of the bread too,
sidelines of good
come in handy.

End of each month
one will see well
for the moment.
When that does come
you will not eat –
too offensive!
And then the war
draws to a close.

IVH 13

His brother's tone
was offensive –
this exists in
imagina-
tion only – with
war still known there
for years, they don't
believe we're done.

Summer dazzles
with it's white lunch –
a good truth does
not see when it's
black like today.
Its character
exactly thus
drawn by the wind.

I said a few
moments ago:
this chicken won't
upset me, and
one cooked like that –
not completely –
things turned morose.
What do you think?

Enter from a
small Berlin trail –
looks to me like
it's gilded well
and succulent –
famous choice to
eat my piece will
reserve myself.

If I were this
chicken I would
hang Guillaume and
be sure to live
a hundred years
and seven – you
enter to stop
from believing.

Known as prophets
of misfortune,
most workmen are
victorious,
but it takes time,
while in the road
rollers dribbled
in disorder.

They who had much
to gain were frank,
and one chicken
per day buys such
an amount for
you and me – so
easy for them
to remember.

They are in the
factories that
pay hooligans
to turn the shells,
while the peasants
you find in the
middle class have
egg on their face.

IVH 14

That tone is done
to break free of
the figure in
the trenches, made
naturally,
likely broken
by what I might
finally say.

All the people
will be Habsbourgs
or in prison.
I thank you for
Senator's goods,
which as you know
did not arrive.
You want salad?

Some lies will be
more trouble but
only women move
the rear one known
as stupid – there
will be more of
your war daydreams.
What do you know?

Truth appeared like
perfect virtue,
not to resist
the plainforms of
will, regretting
unacknowledged
uniforms as
stupid rascals.

Let us admit
when I return
that you never
said that nine-tenths
of the blackened
women smell like
necessary
whores currently.

A few moments
ago you bet
that the war would
last one more year –
this Camembert
tastes like truth to
me, you say, cheese
perhaps. Believe.

Errors often
make the future
truth, laughing at
the one who died.
Defeatists refute
pessimistic
remarks, because
they are brothers.

You listen to
neurasthenic
natural lives;
if one is right
these oranges
that came from Spain
should let us go
to Switzerland.

IVH 15

Thanks, perhaps not,
to our cousin
who ceased to be,
because we dined
one afternoon
and also sent
them the remains
of an orange.

Cousin Adolf
makes me think that
now was not a
time for nice girls
to be private–
time moreover
is badly seen
as family.

Take seven things
and wind them in-
to a ball. Now
come with us as
if knowing we
joined this very
afternoon, said
hours of regret.

For better or
worse, while dining
they will be forced
to eat like pigs.
The third amount,
with courtesy,
is time to in-
vent Switzerland.

If you refuse
to look at the
truth in the face,
your day will be –
let's not think – un-
necessary
after coffee
to astonish.

Nimbly arrived
on the half hour
in front of a
small villa where
the dog kept an
earthenware roof –
even a cat
wouldn't matter.

In other times
winter-roasted
geraniums
were pushed open
in the garden
while running hens
loudly shouted
"I am content!"

It was Annette
who said "Hello,
I am content.
To see, oh yes,
my small . . . call me
older sister . . .
Rather, Annette –
cinema, yes!"

IVH 16

"Enter, Sir," thus
it shouted, but
it was Chinese –
maybe Persian –
enter the air
Kimono girl
hand it to him
right cordially.

To penetrate
pigskins of the
national will,
mostly allied
in that part called
living room, made
more various
than photographs.

Officers with
varied weapons
said it while my
British godson's
eye was blinking.
The General
went straight to a
whisky bottle.

The little boy
in the sport shirt
emerges twice.
We'll go where she
will not lead us.
I only want
one truth: cine-
matography.

I did nothing
but express one
fear, kept silent
to occupy
such a point, ad
infinitum,
left little time
to seek the air.

Therefore, Sir, think
of fifteen years –
and since that age
I would find these
kids who must then
understand which
fine factory
I should include.

It means giving
all of them good
education.
It is not my
fault if present
company made
idiots claim
social lime pits.

Swallowing a
little soup his
older sister
thought it best to
do what added
better over
whisky known as
small impatience.

IVH 17

The beginning:
silence goes one
better, known as
any page, your
interpreters
believe it, known
as the children,
I believe them.

You know that I'm
intuitive.
If you do not
like habitude,
pay attention;
there is always
something older,
like tomorrow.

It is not to
pay the grown well,
that one goes to
the cinema.
It's for polo,
tomorrow, I
take them along.
raising a gift.

What I fear most:
what's known as bad
company – so
much per hour – can't
rely on me.
Older sister,
always wary.
"Pay attention"!

Current satyrs
rely on me:
Captain Anzac.
You have this fact:
to bring himself
so much per hour,
hooligan spas
dispatched by war.

The man and both
charming sisters
travelled by tram.
Should be seen as
honest children –
known as how not
to express some
cause for alarm.

Annette gave her
brother a blow
and blinked her eyes
to bend the coasts.
As when you walk
the grimace is
another of
your true answers.

What can one play?
When young imp's gone
and Pathé's owl
is never geese.
Your impatience
took you along
in ignorance.
They kept silent.

IVH 18

Not far from them
a thick crowd ran
in front of the
blackened pavement –
they kept silent.
A catch sits down
knowing that this
will have no place.

If you start to
say it again,
this well known word,
knowing that cheer
does not prevent
reason from your
having much more
real affection.

My well known eye –
not to leave your
only unit –
will not conceal
the children, you
idiot. Go
enter, which one
will be wanted?

Now they cry in
front of the world –
places rented
like this, you think?
Orchestras with
less openness
let a little
runt lead them all.

Less orchestras
than nice velvet
armchairs, Annette
consequently
was then moved to
tears, discreetly –
the small girl made
her leave on cue.

Without their chief,
the little one
behind was made
to reform two
trout, each one a
little further
from where one might
make family.

According to
the probable
age of this one,
the remainder
of spectators
were British men –
a noisy mass
in the hen house.

One cigarette
or a candy
half sucked – on the
third parquet floor;
they played the Serb
national an-
them – at this hour
the people rose.

IVH 19

Reprobative
anti-clerics
without shocking
did not have his
value shortened
beside English
soldiers whistling
their convictions.

Everyone was
so content, but
few middle-class
Frenchmen under-
stood – including
which, thanks to their
instructions, were
seen with the cooks.

The armies had
their good life in
the trenches – then
two or three things
reignited –
relief lamps whence
the format of
newspapers came.

Polo said "It's
not too early."
It was constrained:
pretending not
to feel its age.
Two old ladies
behind the hen.
"Bet them to place."

This then: Le Havre,
home of horse race,
not the same as
the day before
yesterday, one
patent moment
offered the kids
scandalous laugh.

Two old ladies
did not take the
trouble to scorn –
they kept silent –
the night was done
in again by
one document
on horsemanship.

Indifferent,
disappointed
consternations
of black horses
danced on the white
silver screen where
the foam then slowed
and flew away.

Softly, above
the hedge, all drawn
up and greeting
themselves, withdrawn
in their stable –
a reel lime pit
no matter what
the public knows.

In spite of the
storm he arrived
in the face of
those who respect
decency: an
amount of some
uniformly
beautiful skirts.

English carried
one tightened thigh,
so they did not
rise as known points –
"Very well, I
alone thank you.
This time, we walk
along the sea."

Broad waves embarked
upon the dam.
as if pouring
water from a
small pitcher in-
to a basin with
no cosmetic
improvements thought.

Ah yes, it is
thus drawn by wind;
it looked to be
exactly creased,
as such he had
remembered a
beautiful girl
with little chest.

IVH 20

Although it's just
a little punt,
the sea shook the
oarlocks while they
dribbled in the
roads of two or
three ships floating
in disorder.

One sheep, Miss Weeds,
of course, going
down to extremes
often meant that they
had sought another
barometer.
Perhaps they are
here for transport.

New Cinema
often goes to
France the first time.
And you like that?
An amateur,
interesting,
accustomed to
keeping silent.

Abruptly turns
astonished masks
to lives applied
to its stupor.
What do you hate?
Can one know that,
if he makes a
discovery?

IVH 21

One personal
question murmured
that it thought of
only thought, then
fear, abruptly
realizing
just how much he
preferred the truth.

It appeared to
him, I added,
starting higher,
this very thought
that can't be seen.
Relationship
with cinema?
I cannot see.

This Anglican
and commonplace
reminder: white
beside the girl
of far away
war understood –
imagined it
includes the heart.

Rapture employed
a uniform,
enormously
expensive forms
suited his charms,
includes (approved)
the same terms as
he dared to ask.

Look! Ornaments
hung like darkness
with long panes in
black scraps which wind
will agitate
diverting face –
quiet counters
supporting night.

Deserted some
two consumers –
disfigured, yet
faces in time –
little person's
single coffee
engraving their
long heavy time.

The harshly drawn
concern of course
took a dislike
to the large French
bobbies – pleasant
beauties and young –
insufficient
retrospective.

All young people
until now had
embraced rancid
adrogynes and
poor insipid
clerks fermenting
in brownish milk
but always fresh.

IVH 22

By their bathtub
comforts, suburbs
delirious
with lengthened hair,
feeling like wrists
with lowered sound,
their eyes being
of a small race.

Discrete signs of
virility –
not the black fleece
of oozing slaves –
their company
in sleeping bags
only wanted
reluctant babes.

The hand tightened,
realizing
suddenly he's
no more there than
when he left on
the passing tram
returning to
tomorrow's rose.

The pavement light
testified to
some interest
in the coffee;
methodically
paid the fatty
female owner's
wavered return.

In the small rain
that startled night,
he did not make
their attention –
face too wet to
fall against his
crushed rollers in
plated darkness.

Sometimes whiteness
burst through a wave,
swept its surface,
thought of something
very remote,
periodic,
drew on a wire
revolving light.

Its life was all
untied – nothing
found but more parts –
looked at childhood
with tedious
faculty – a
disaster, some
contrite studies.

Unpleasant love,
student jokes, a-
bominable
deprivation,
all functioning
like sheets of joy
or militant
service remarks.

IVH 23

A bouquet of
fireworks spanning
the scattered sea
waves enthus-
astically,
seized by sudden
outbursts of blunt
tragic echoes.

Quick excessive
measure remains
an army of
one drawn by its
vulgar crossings,
less than one day's
decoration,
always brilliant.

Because he could
not swim, met storms
and cyclones, books
and quick shipwrecks
some sour vomit
in the lead sky
of his childhood
calm under fire.

His own life flat,
sight mobilized,
the beautiful
Miss Weed's movement
only engaged
small miseries
which had consumed
a fatherland.

According to
the measurement
summarized, such
easy release
of its thanks means
sure arrival –
takes it all in
to the fair girl.

Disasters could
not answer what
they twisted, would
want you to see
the length of the
maritime wind.
That's why I tell
you these stories

Cinema burned
the boulevard
installed ten years
ago – long time,
my mother's gone –
large galleries
did not yet know
to be themselves.

My woman and
daughters-in-law
and a brother
had disappeared
then finished three
disgusting days
at the hour of
silent collapse.

IVH 24

Here is what I
discovered at
this very hour:
one idiot
thought comment still
accountable,
another track,
not the whole wire.

Children's useful
remarks became
necessary.
Better a son
with his whole face
interesting
than stories told
of families.

I want to say
"confused entry,"
also to say
strong young person,
older than me –
pretty besides –
there was always
a certain face.

Resemblance in
a glance between
the two of them –
fugitive head,
the body's pace
unexamined –
small centres and
the true one's pearls.

Conversation
comes with subject
official to
primitive time.
Excessive white
teeth well planted,
long legs also –
but those full hips?

These savages
have dogs to kill
my cats, turned sour
by their hatred
of the action.
Authorizing
me to make this
will be easy.

Accompanied
relationships
would be foolish
to leave, as if
baring gifts born
differently
with rare shades of
generous thoughts.

They arrived at
the granting of
Holy Address –
pretexts passed to
agitation –
in addition
the night had grown
a silent wind.

IVH 25

One bump above,
naturally
the deserted
rollers advanced
to make the tea,
and the wind was
not little but
very little.

One cannot speak
engaged to drink
better coffee
in this life of
hostilities
and continued
interruptions
of appearance.

Because London
did not engage
the dressmaker
it is certain
they did not hide
their modest Dad's
alcoholic
situation.

In front of him
it was easy
to conclude that
two or three small
holidays or
stays of summer
misery in
the countryside.

Sit cross-legged
in a profile
preceding the
movements of the
reality –
tender and soft,
the flexible
light of her smile.

Movements away
from the sea and
the sure curve of
street-corner whores
recomposed as
sick desire felt
centred on the
downtown markets.

Discretion seen
half hip half calf
above the full
embrasure of
a door, its head
an umbrella
deployed to say:
"Come, you're cherished."

When asked again:
"Why make surprise?"
How to begin?
Continuous
Monotony.
Chants can only
explain why things
are made so dear.

IVH 26

Sulphate layer's
useful method
entered the shop
covered by a
sympathetic
handkerchief – a
generous nerve
in its cold train.

After the blow
of his native
visitor, the
comprehensive
operations
were explained as
requested by
dreadful people.

To tell her that
she had been called
stupid agreed
to believe your
woman's insane
old bones, dust on
the head of the
masterpieces.

In spite of its
contempt for the
concerns of the
occult, as his
old friend told him,
bonesetters' sad
histories mend-
ed broken bones.

The medicine
aggravated
certain witches'
conversations.
The guarantor,
wearied, conceals
certain fires of
the enchantment.

Dividing books
into sheets, time
turns any page
into silence
to feed the fix
of the old men
who did not seem
to be evil.

Quotidian
Athens will have
demolished the
Parthenon – one
hope bombarded,
the unpleasant
made civilized.
Defenders laughed.

King Constantine,
germanophile,
glances, points to
the allied cause.
You have today
nothing but fear
infinitum
to seek silence.

IVH 27

Today you have
the odd air known
as nevermore –
elemental,
like habitude,
surely not if
something changed there
for no reason.

You know that we're
under almost
idiotic
violence: the
intuitive.
You have the odd
air of today,
it must be love.

My forgiveness
makes excuses
excessively.
To say that I
simply wanted
to find insult's
strange idea
under the seat.

Your reaction
to cathartic
psychology
proves to be love.
I am rightly
known as insane
and won't prevent
the card-index.

After all if
I were in love
it would look like
having a young
person seeing
a blonde married
girl – or is this
where I return?

You can't sell love –
spiritual,
like the traitor
it laughed at – large,
but always French –
mere affection:
where theatre's
municipal.

Then we added
a filter of
inspiration
known as today's
pleonasm
intended to
prepare you for
the natural.

Though the filter
does not love you,
today's laughter
was found to be
a little bit
empty in the
head, sometimes not
very conscious.

IVH 28

Favourite dis-
tractions: middle-
class men, avid
pigs, rough workmen,
dried hearts, dumb sheep –
a tram along
the horror of
its empty self.

A long walk through
quark-working thirds
where the space-quays
and share-machines
abominate –
a world of work
cogitated
by activity.

Large sweating dis-
proportionate
requests appear
to laugh – no joke –
operates quite
naturally
everywhere
without despair.

Obstinate in
its regret, love
does not have some
Hamlet tell a
silent female
customer to
seriously
seek adventure.

It is never
one woman, one
woman – even
your stories of
one woman – what
he said to me:
It is always
the same old thing.

In silence we
examined the
watch dial like
a singular
ordinary
shell turn into
extra matter
mother-of-pearl.

Your back-story
this moment comes
right after sound,
never before,
asking your news.
This is not an
affectation
of his office.

An empty head
was found in the
street, not very
conscious of its
existence, judged
from whence he walks
by one God to
display Himself.

IVH 29

The monsters of
catastrophe
engender shame –
burst on the ground
the rare ones drop
heavy water
reflecting fall's
germination.

Perverse shades and
overpowered
contempt maintained
the horror of
his heart – children
delighted in
factories for
the repulsion.

Insolent pro-
letarians –
rabble in caps –
absorbed brutal
torturers of
decent people,
dirty drunkards,
seditious kids.

Brothels crawling
with nausea,
nearer to hell
than their public
image, causing
linens in the
human race to
develop Him.

Hatred in his
heart caused him to
make spectacle
of repugnant
disorders which
surface in him
without speaking
to pacifists.

Cargo liners
on slow water
basins offered
beautiful blow
where stone quays at
rest caused rain to
fall on the pained
snails of sadness.

Like pearls after
the storm, human
mistresses
show themselves, stuck
under lessons
of various
apparently
free continents.

The paddle boats
moored along those
estuaries
quickly stopped there,
resting unex-
plained, with all three
abstract sailors
up on the bridge.

IVH 30

The field of fair
had just traversed
the street, in its
arms a number
of red living
rooms times fifteen,
to the spoils in
his laugh only.

An antago-
nistic mirror
now reflected
its own image,
limply hanging
far in front which,
by abstraction,
regards one frieze.

These disorders
rang up nothing
indefinite
against the sound
entry of stores
of loneliness –
apparently
without thinking

He believed and
was reminded
that various
incidents of
horror, famous
and terrible,
now burn in their
large galleries.

Two astonished
customers, while
considering
your suffering,
returned the milk –
just thirteen years
short of morning's
entered constraints.

My brother Christ
makes a point of
celebrating
birthdays every
fifty years, and
in the ev'ning
pretends to shave
two things downtown.

A small dinner
for family
does not feel aged
obviously –
inviting some
colleagues to think
about the hour –
not the banquets.

With art and strength
the well-informed
started to soap
the crown up front,
while victory's
entrusted with
my offer to
await the day.

A well informed
imbecile had
many walking
illusions, while
including that
thing known here as
serious fun,
just to vomit.

That's one good thing
left of winter –
another risk
between us for
at least the time
you still manage
to split hairs of
silent facials.

Please understand
that he had switched
his host on a
divergence, which
gave the above
book to him when
it poured water
in the basin.

Important things
not to get stuffed:
an amount of
cranium one
thinks important,
everything
despite our deep
insanity.

IVH 31

He rectified
the line, cut the
moustache, brushed the
jacket, approved
of each themselves,
paid by each mouth
smiling in the
cosmetic street.

At the bottom
the word France is
synonymous
with Germany.
Poor idiot
just undergone
thought improvements –
beautiful moods.

Cold climate is
unusual
which makes the wind
very merry –
could not feel his
legs or swallow
the water for
fifteen minutes.

They exchanged quick
remarks, tightened
the owner's hand,
already there
when it arrived,
benign excess
made his language
superior.

IVH 32

Nantout, Sacqueville,
Duplanchet and
their ladies at
war with the wire.
The men one spoke
about carried
very large trains
around wormwood.

After Bernard
the future way
of iron and
joint safeties used
the perfidy
which was made for
fish to be built
into railroads.

The discussion
was with ardour –
a series of
invectives a-
gainst oppression –
everyone
agreed, good claims
found their own steps.

Male and female
elements that
count around their
alternate lines
combined order
and sat between
the general
conversation.

Drowned poisonings
were caused by the
bottles lined up
under a flood
of unscented
shallot vinegar
and these happy
scented branches.

When one started
speaking gallant
war, his hairy
neighbour, the young
person, was not
satisfied with
choice, and would
not even explain.

His wound often
scorned the war each
month to explain
alcoholic
indicators –
carried monthly
toasts – fifty years
of brilliant mood.

The victory
of France and its
Allies will hang,
accompanied
by various
chatterings caught
by exposure
to telegraphy.

IVH 33

The Tsar with the
Eiffel Tower.
Espionage
without the wire.
Telegraphy
of certain facts.
The cathedral
player piano.

While courting his
sister-in-law
today, the low
speaking voice would
be funny if
more air were un-
known tomorrow,
Don't look at it!

I drank too much!
Please do not joke
at this moment.
Funny or odd?
Not singular.
Listen rather
gently to who
would be in love.

And you yourself
would not have much
affection or
indeed include
allusion to
the one who's known
but can't be clear
or understood.

In any case
you imagine
the stupid one's
small bag of bones
that isn't done,
and however
kind beautiful
girls in the flesh.

We continue
to assist this
discussion of
certain moral
disorder of
time's origin
which ruins all
demonstration.

If Kings were not
also cuckolds
the family
dissociates
to exception
believing them
all to be drunk
from the bottom.

These too are old
women liking
odd animals,
although they took
the money so
finally – tall
stories swallowed
one uniform.

IVH 34

These girls' backstreets
passionately
continuing
to underline
occasional
impressive trails
with two times left
to see its base.

You intend to
marry him? This
very moment?
Old sacrament
impossibly
eccentric – in
any case not
even engaged.

Things cannot think.
At this moment
the company
weathers marriage.
This large person
in question, still
exceptional –
virgin, I think.

If I dare the
large blonde girl to
shine her soft hair –
who made me lose
my direction –
whence I advanced
precisely for
the train of wines.

I'm here to tell
you I believe,
advanced towards
the talking air.
What does he want
with these little
ladies? Better
conversation?

I leave you, Rose,
if not morose,
Brother sitting
down beside him
ruffled, telling
strange histories
of beautiful
tenderized blow.

Let us go then
you and I to
simply say that
those two children
at the Sunday
cinema are
completely un-
natural too.

The bastards tell
me silly things
of their others
and the wonders
of their even
affectations –
they're finally
just the plain truth.

Because he could
draw the charts and
drew them as the
end of days, which
then fell to him –
because he got
dressed in colours
initially.

The first vital
forces, in fact,
to marry with
hastened dirty
cats and coaches
and surrounded
itself with small
ignored genius.

As soon as he
intended to,
the character
to whom you speak
precipitates
outside howling –
the door to the
garden opened.

Starts to gain con-
siderable
sums then, with ease:
cargo liners,
garlic barges,
and onion trains
of condensed milk
they could enjoy.

IVH 35

Then resold his
paste-ups to some
crass commercial
gardens, which then
populate with
Gruyere cream and
large croquets of tom
cats, a goat and

a rich peacock.
Bought a villa,
jewels, furs, top
hats, pendulums,
and well-worn glass-
ware to preserve –
adulterates
naturally.

Lastly they bought
all that they can't
formally scorn;
now the richest
carafe stoppers,
twice charged
under the weight
of animals.

Known as the good
ceremonial
pot of fortune,
happy persons
dine without us,
making half-turns
benevolent
between the legs.

IVH 36

The shoe-makers
were born with black
lachrymal moods –
nor did they learn
patriotic
triumph over
economic
orphan brothers.

It was for them
however that
two of his guest
connections kept
the bottom scorned
all his life – the
financial ground
had not been French.

Because boarders
did not escape
to laugh at me,
or in any case
swallow this neck,
I believed in
gastronomy
and victory.

Stupefied but
unwanted. He
one day made a
cooker, because
each evening
precipitates
claims towards the
kitchen's answers.

Years of unpaid
ideas in
engaged legions
against nothing
that important –
rubbing his hands,
with his wife's head
in the furnace.

The family
understood that
necessary
services threw
grated pepper –
bitter silence
caused a great en-
thusiasm.

Cancelling the
subject did not
establish pride
in digestion
or irritate
like small droppings
nor calm my gross
sponge with soft words.

Only this one
very expensive
declaration
finally came
to make a turn
yesterday and
they did not run
to invite us.

IVH 37

It was the same
first day sea, one
part of winter
according to
astronomers,
advanced autumn,
rather sclerosed,
and anchylosed.

The horizon
at the same time
methodical,
liquefied but
industrial,
very gently
inflated waves
burst with rollers.

Helena's hands
were love's final
declaration,
contained under
table legs in
terms never bored
with the back of
her lovely neck.

The rain and rant
of the wind in-
flated desire,
strangled it like
some cranial
capsule, stomach
emptied, kneaded
like a hunger.

Poisoned husband's
kidneys, entrails
increasingly
more beautiful –
through two woven
thicknesses, cloth
materials
of its trousers.

His hands pressed
osseous, seemed
thin like a boy's,
was flesh between
its bottoms of
felt, like the wool
and physio –
logical walk.

But then the calf
went up to the
thigh pensively
finding the width
of the hips and
the probable
firmness of the
buttocks only.

He kept silent,
released his legs,
withdrew his hands,
still raised his eyes,
looked at this man
who seemed to take
seriously
the love transformed.

IVH 38

Love: not even
a "business,"
something of a
sentimental
tragedy of
the voyage of
landscape – only
one element.

However con-
vincing, it could
lose its urgent
virginity –
shivering love
unaware of
anything – not
of my exits.

Only a moving
Frenchy, but all
the same a man,
again took the
hand to him and
cherished it, then
the idea came
to embrace him.

Landscape appeared to
cause talk by an
examined, pre-
liminary
width of hardly
agreed upon
separated
coffee tables.

Moreover I
will arrange that
the horizon,
already night and
known, was exact,
but not easy
to practice on
the boulevard.

Black rain spread out,
cold wind and sea
continued to
break, a lantern
tumbled down, top
to bottom of
the boulevard –
a scrap of night.

It was a tram
besides, I joked,
headlights turning
into muddy
clouds, weather stopped
to decipher
the horizon
unsatisfied.

Astonished to
crush his wet lips
against opened
mouths, of modest
hands between the
balustrade and
boulevard
towards a crowd.

IVH 39

Thirteen women
separated
from the beach by
speakers, embraced
towards the pressed
rollers like the
shoulders of a
man with closed eyes.

The Frenchy looked
at it with fear,
when it got clear,
which proved it was
simply that it
moved away from
him and started
to go slowly.

They were to be
re-examined
not embraced, the
following day –
the hand tightened,
first politely;
thus they went in
further silence.

He vaguely tried
to lengthen the
time of this found
handshake but it
escaped like a
brook from the sea,
emerged stumbling
against the night.

Old memories
of vacuum-packed
dignity pre-
vented damaged,
more insincere
kisses from their
revivified
collapsing taste.

A flexible
animal which
its Master seeks
to love – until
its much older
steps had led – pressed
against his first
thought without sleep.

It entered with
the stupefied
aspect of an
epileptic
choir on the ground
who'll be killed by
those gangsters' dis-
located evil.

"Ah, the rough ones."
A dog perhaps
would be stripped or
diverted by a
stiff decency.
Ah, the bastards,
perhaps naked,
soon found broken.

IVH 40

This Sunday in
front of the door
against a grid
supporting the
beautiful street,
he'd washed his hands,
lowered his eye-
lids, and waited.

The small vain one
murmured by far,
seeing that its
too soft tears came
floating, then dried
with winter wind.
I am more than
beautiful now.

Because today
only loving
was delicious,
I cannot guess
the other times,
children laughed in
the middle of
their murmured birds.

I tapped his cheek
then abruptly
one went away –
he's an idi-
otic boy-scout.
"Where is Polo?"
It is not the
only sorrow.

Perhaps it is
necessary
that I say to
your sister that
I'll take a long
walk this Sunday,
coast to coast, deep
in the forest.

He was too large.
Carry my child
a few metres,
with his small arms
tightened against
gray metal sheets.
Do not disturb,
or stop the tram.

I don't envy
your dust up or
your will to have
cold parents with
obstructions to
the cinema.
So they would want
to make small talk?

I want to go
to a forest
that's very cold.
In this case we'll
take the tram in
the other known
direction, smart
with the small girl.

IVH 41

They wait for the
tram a long time,
then they entered
between flint trees,
split the forest
under their feet.
The extreme cold
required laughter.

You're not too cold?
Quite true. When I'm
happy with you
it makes me hot.
When you're with me
I do not think
with the hardness
of colder times.

You're unhappy?
I'm not very
happy either.
It's not the same.
But you are still
older sister
ever constant,
too small, too young.

In a little
more than one year
I want to have
taught myself some
new age English
conversations –
only then will
I marry you.

I do not seek
to be often
re-examined,
stopped and upset
with our cane in
layers of dried sheets,
very dead they
could not answer.

If I were a
little more than
one year older,
would you marry
me moreover?
The English one,
slow to answer,
tried to catch up.

Initially
astonished, what
invitation
does she like? Will
we speak again
about cinema
impatiently
in dulcet tones?

All the time I
think of you while
waiting for the
Sunday exit.
Then I find you
beautiful, I
murmured, works then
flees while running.

IVH 42

He turned over
and saw his poor
frightened girlfriend
on the dead sheets.
Her awkwardness,
so unpleasant,
stopped to note your
condescension.

It appeared a
little pity
murmured quickly,
after running
up a small flame,
his words drawn in,
the night something
so amazing.

Sulky children
should not prevent
disgusting dreams
because of their
length who really
must believe the
existence of
Father Christmas.

Since it is not
possible to
think all the time
of the English,
a malignant
air moreover,
one looked at it
with tenderness.

That's not true, it's
not possible.
Could you become
a spy, as with
what you told me
the other day:
add wonder to
the cinema.

You remember
you wanted to
become a spy.
If you married
me, how could you
become a spy?
or abruptly
discover me?

Attention stopped
a flame which lights
do not prevent –
two breaths, very
extreme wonder –
appears your friend
has married one
poisonous man.

They laughed and howled,
which laughter pushed
a wheelbarrow
charged with deadwood.
Still it shouted –
it was frightened:
a prisoner
always of war.

IVH 43

You did not come
to lunch Sunday.
I was anxious,
waited one hour,
since we didn't
have any more
news. I'm running
with what sends me.

Dinner was not
open, nor was
it denied, when
read politely
while yawning, raised
the master key
awaiting the
required entrance.

He wants to leave
you in your juice,
like they say. He
believes that you're
annoyed because
questions asked to
make advances
amount the worst.

Although I was
annoyed, but not
insane, I was
occupied by
what does not look
after all like
what upset the
glass connection.

No sooner do
I break the legs
of one child, does
my unhappy
elder brother
come to me with
a tapeworm that
will not finish.

The cinema
has no more right
to remove sen-
iority
than carry out
a statement that
resembles those
with whom we play.

Could have warned us.
Warned me also
to annoy you.
I am stupid.
Good. Let that pass.
I regret this
confidence of
damaged feelings.

Please excuse my
indiscretion.
I often do
not represent
myself that well.
Undoubtedly she's
married, found a
beautiful world.

IVH 44

There are heaps of
things which one would
never suspect.
For example,
I don't find you
beautiful or
even pink. Did
you doubt it then?

You make me walk
from time to time
if only to
be difficult –
supposing your
beastly remark
was deemed to be
necessary.

I wrote: "Until
this moment we
did nothing but
make fun of you
announcing your
permission for
the festivals –
which made us laugh.

Pleasure reduced
my proportions
on Christmas to
an optimist's
We wanted to
simply announce
that Charles had come
to dine with us.

Who are these two
children that I
take every
Sunday to the
cinema? I
know nothing of
their New Year's gifts
nor their Christmas.

But don't forget
to make like my
brother, simple
intelligent
invitations
being tested
according to
these riding boots.

Then Monday rose
shortly after
diction entered
the door sounding
as if it was
being tested
by the use of
pretty women.

Then much later
the Frenchwoman
met my sister-
in-law – the feel
of leather was
a little late
for a mouth with
eyes of butter.

IVH 45

I saw him in
front of his soup,
that good hot soup
which burns, and then
saw the plants whole,
the blurred smoke grew
ceremonies
under craters.

The smoke escaped
from its known place
to be present
in the form of
an appearance
evoked by the
prestige of the
heavy magic.

He saw this man
he hardly knew
who occupied
the open space
opposite him,
his arm was raised,
motionless, a
spoon in the hand.

Astonished, we
observed it and
saw, suspended
from the furnace
bronze towards the
infamous dawn,
unpleasant thoughts
plunged in the fog.

The voice required
an object which
had been stirred up
and manufactured –
remained in style
on the chimney
between two of
the orange trees.

There was no shade,
no dining room
with flowers – truth
was no phantom,
a phantom much
heavier, thick-
ness of the past
coagulates.

Memory, the
phosphorescent
trace of being
deceased, a clot
remembering
another shade.
Neither friend nor
superior.

Knowledge has full
feelings passed from
wedding bells to
democratic
silence wherein
each man is told
not to worry
about the end.

Quite simply May
felt molten to
the hotel trade –
snow availed tu-
berculosis –
and perhaps he
liked his mother's
sudden decrease.

His wife returned
and repulsion
abruptly tests
the forces fire
devoured, gently
maintained the cause
of disordered
conversation.

His aversion
for much tightened
embarrassment
admits disgust
for something
glossier than
demi-mondaine
significance.

Perceiving the
elements as
too heavy to
discover, the
host understood
that it was a
tactic of alms'
fallen increase.

IVH 46

Providing for
its part only
some growls, without
appreciable
cheese, it still smelled
better because the
apple-brandy
completely cleared.

You see, there are
some things of which
I have horror
over all: Jews,
Freemasons, trade
unions, teachers,
conscious workmen,
organized lists.

Freedom, Social
democracy,
equality,
fraternity –
and the Bourbons?
Look at their nose!
All that makes me
want to vomit.

It would not be
necessary
for France to save
itself from much
disorder and
decrepitude,
to rise and pour
another glass.

IVH 47

Adolf was the
first nobody
they saw, with his
quartz and his large
behind. Charles, his
brother, arrived
last, his face was
the mask of joy.

Thérèse crossed her
legs and showed the
lower part of
her calves sheathed in
leather laced high.
She had always
loved her nephew's
tight behaviour.

An ear fixed at
the centre of
its memory
precipitates
agitated
quiet shoulder
disturbances
in an armchair.

His parallel
warlike exploits
chattered in the
distance until
the Swiss cousin
made the bubble
sit down with the
solid hubbub.

Listen to the
image without
disturbing its
enchanted curves
in accordance
with these rumbles
of intended
obfuscation.

Given lustre
contrary to
the dog which will
upset its own
reflection by
drinking the clear
water which tries
to reflect it.

Against the wall
of cranium,
a flower of
marvellous and
translucent flesh,
echoes start by
exhausting the
informal talk.

Language, with its
small wet fleshy
animal which
they all embraced,
leaves its tepid
bath and struggles
again with its
flexible best.

IVH 48

The wind slips, born
between their lips,
separates their
faces like knives,
things one finds in
bilingual
handbooks, for those
who never speak.

About transport,
and of the good
war, eyes close on
the cloth of the
uniform and
its fingers are
contracted to
take it again.

To embrace the
weather – very
cold – is to come
home, is very
reasonable,
doesn't answer
cold questions or
brutal requests.

She went through the
dining room and
spliced her brother's
gestures by his
small, invented,
translucently
objective eyes
without thinking.

Take their walk, go
slowly, it is
that beautiful –
each incident
excused itself
to discover
their ears could not
make discretion.

Sometimes Penny
laughed, constrained through
pure lack of vague
astonishment –
enthusias-
tic soldiers know
heroism
when they see it.

"Pack up" was a
phrase which they had
learned from the good
newspaper, but
naturally,
adversaries
reflected are
frightened comrades.

Hostilities
seldom enrich
known demented
cowards' murmured
counterpart vo-
cabularies.
"Some people will
exaggerate."

IVH 49

One would have to
cut the hands off
little children,
burn cathedrals,
to find this small
discussion, strong,
diverting, not
just be dismissed.

One could expect
to hear the most
scandalous re-
marks, the most ex-
travagant view,
but this time it
exceeded all
point measurement.

Men with enough
insurance gave
him the right to
speak all the same.
Which concludes you're
excusable, and
very often
condescending.

Adolf faces
foreign questions,
strategies and
policies of
consternation.
The life of men
a little more
animated.

One spoke about
things finally
having been spoiled –
some satisfied
recognition
of his triumph,
more to divert
the naive ones.

The discipline
was very severe
if one returned
to England – they
were examined,
undoubtedly, and
would be written
after the war.

He did not want
to be done in
by what was oft
called illusions –
it was finished,
radical, stuck
absolutely
like ocean death.

The absence of
the same stone shells,
the same top wood,
a wave tears one
off from them and
absorbs, trembling,
some other rock,
some other ship.

Ridiculous,
it would be lost
again, hung up
with the shell of
his delicate
ear, absorbed at
the bottom of
his memory.

Of all the swell
catastrophes,
the opaque mass
of misfortunes
of the world, this
separation
would be lost and
undistinguished.

After dinner
came the guests, an
image of a
future meeting
in peaceful times –
and history
will know the thick leg
of its novel.

He sat in an
armchair, glass in
hand, smiling with
contempt. Then each
was assembled
to watch many
sleeping children
be tenderized.

IVH 50

Charles disappears,
at once charmed by
some young female,
draws a chair close
to politely
offer Champagne,
splendid toys and
a fixed armchair.

There is a fire
which, ignited,
passes close to
some children, who
extend and share
each of their burns
with all that is
propagated.

After this we
will start again
to play the old
phonograph, we
will dance, certain
that these moments
mean that it will
not stop snowing.

It is often
impossible
for me to speak
to you about
the parents of
these completely
little children
kept so silent.

IVH 51

In front of his
coffee with milk,
Christmas passed with
extreme slowness,
without putting
its usual
spirit in the
same way too much.

The newspapers
online did not
precipitate
abstractedly –
yesterday's blinds
carried evening,
felt light headed,
muddled the brain.

We alerted
a small vacuum,
even answered
that there was a
certain something
which was going
to arrive the
day of the fire.

He started to
soak his bread in
a cup full of
brownish juice, but
the eyes of the
surface of the
negligence were
very anxious.

Finally he
worried about
the butter flood
and gave up the
quick dip and the
official peace –
a statement of
the upset day.

With the large lunch
as with the small
he balked at food
and was never
afraid to take
a laxative –
a late fifteen
year old service.

There were suspect
bastard nerves on
the tablecloth –
noone believed
they would return –
a departure
from which he'd not
sing any more.

He had medals,
decorations,
crosses, badges.
He was frank and
hierarchic.
But it was not
possible to
out think the fire.

The rose fire was
examined with
more interest,
of a volume
rather gray and
important but
not useful in
the afternoon.

The lieutenant
draws morals from
this history:
discipline – not
the moment to laugh –
discipline: frank
explanations
control return.

The emptied hand
does not consist
of small British
virgins, "Courage
my boy!" as the
Captain tightens
the difficult
Entente Cordiale.

He rests against
a post, stumbles,
he would now need
his cane to go.
He sweats. He must
finish his day
at the office.
You drank too much.

IVH 52

Today is the
day when there is
precisely too
much dirty work –
you should return
to your premise,
after it should
be looked into.

You do not have
the well known air,
which leaves to grow
dark, and harms night,
there is also
a fog pile, bits
of larvae which
stick to themselves.

The quiet re-
verberators
will find a well
of knowledge in
a man of true
conscience if the
work is to be
completed soon.

It is enough
to insist and
drink one or two
rounds in company.
The car slips by
towards the port.
It's a long way
to circumvent.

IVH 53

Days ago, when
there was much work,
military
motor vehicles
were placed at his
disposal – one
will never see
the end of it.

The gods sleep on
the quays – the fog
is a sleeping
bag because its
phosphorescent
envelope will
never see the
end of a dream.

It's a long way
to lengthy dreams
of disgusting
tapeworms which can't
finish any
white mass and its
passing Red Cross
boat-hospital.

He is challenged,
he begs, argues
and will not pass.
The footbridges in
the ship retract.
Second sentry
inserted like a
motionless nail.

The car stops, it
does not pass. It
will never pass.
He looks at lit
port-holes, and
the silhouettes
which go and come
on the bridges.

This appears not
to disturb the
sleep of its clear
reading, even
as certain rose
propellers beat
the water and
fly towards town.

It seems to him
that the car must
traverse each point
of space one by
one remaining
motionless in
the centre of
their *derrières*.

Then suddenly
houses full of
people passing
the lamps and panes,
even a tram,
as of coffees,
the restaurants
and urinals.

IVH 54

The following
day it was learned
that the other
boat-hospital
was torpedoed
by a German
majority
of submarines.

It appeared that
only one of
the passengers
had been saved and
a shipwreck is
not difficult
to imagine
initially.

The women and
children were always
accustomed to
catastrophes
and disasters –
people escape
in obvious
healthier times.

This body, this
face, this hope, these
eyes, these teeth were
not well arranged –
the healthy sign
of the firmness
of its times: Safe,
alive again.

This appeared so
obvious that
it could never
divert him from
his project – one
stupid German
vituperates
necessity.

Cruelty has
certain courage –
a beautiful
audacity
that comes with few
sympathetic
customers whose
love is retained.

After lunch he
took the old tram
and went to the
cemetery.
It stopped in front
of English tombs,
so he looked at
the regiments.

Being informed
raised his shoulders,
went slowly senior,
decorated
with characters,
acknowledging
himself frankly
sick of his rank.

IVH 55

One afternoon
we listened to
the hard winter
escorted by
warships conveyed
by two smiling
complementary
appreciations.

The wind always
blew, and the trees
were only hung
with the preserved
crosses – pickled,
engraved with the
artificial
granite flagstone.

Some flowers bore
the gilded names
of her mother,
her sister-in-
law, and his wife,
immobilized
by naked heads
in front of stones.

He knew well on
the one hand with
nothing to say,
the late ones are
sizeable, but
he believed that
when one dies it's
for a long time.

He was alone
in the cold, but
did not request
or discover
with crossed hands that
he was signed, which
did not prevent
him from crying.

He cried during
ten minutes of
such motionless
bodies, without
dating the sobs,
overlapping,
moved away, its
walk continued.

It was very
long in the cold,
his face resigned,
reading the in-
scriptions, student
of the dates and
relationships –
the last dispersed.

Two grave-diggers
exercising
their trade approached
one very fresh coffin
in a lengthened
pit because my
convalescence
is now done with.

IVH 56

He thought he was
criticizing
the epitaphs
at the end of
the alley in
a box with such
ground swell as would
not suit him well.

Even when his
destination
did not stumble,
he was looking
at laughter for
the first time – it
was surprising,
immediate.

They felt constrained,
then appeared to
make a bit of
otherwise o-
bligatory
atmosphere to
draw up between
human reports.

You do not know
who it is that
one buries there
only to re-
duce what remained
of procession
if ever asked
to sacrifice.

Comic singers
of the Madness-
ratios were
funny – it's life.
Their labour was
emitting phil-
osophical
song reflexions.

My lieutenant
supported the
funny silence
only, those of
the cinema,
moving away
from a fast and
sure final step.

A single blow
of the villa's
doorbell revealed
it was indeed
New Year's Day which
beckoned to him
by greeting them
to make entry.

I was truly
astonished that
it embraced me.
Should I make tea?
Quite hot with rum?
You would be drunk.
Swallowed good for
this cold practice.

IVH57

Is it true you
had real fun the
other ev'ning?
Embrace me now,
I offer you
a spearmint tea,
astonished by
the silent house.

Was it me you
came to see then?
During the known
holidays? You
don't remember?
Was it for that
that you embraced
me all the time?

I remember
not knowing if
I kissed you much –
all the time – but
they weren't really
serious, you
were probably
drunk or married.

Do you have a
girlfriend? Maybe
a connection
with a married
woman? Women
of passage? Hens?
Will you go straight
to Galleons?

You make me walk.
I know that with
my small sister
you are often
very correct.
You are never
vicious, don't have
the head for it.

You don't want me
to tell the truth.
I am without
dirty defects –
pure like mother.
Amazement turned
to compassion.
That was funny.

I look on in
twisted silence –
you tell laughing
stories alive
with media
anguish. It is
not possible,
they were obsessed.

This winter I
was there, in love
with English, but
very extremely,
and finally,
in short, they
said: you cannot
sleep together.

IVH 58 (coda)

There was no hope
that a reading
customer could
leave this thick and
cold silence. She
shivered and rose
again looking
to go for coal.

She put water
once in the hot
water bottle
which could not sing
any more while
the new she-cat
slept in its fur
behind the stove.

Egoistic
particulars
raised their eyes to
look across the
old window prints
of falling snow –
the street had turned
completely white.

Alone, she crossed
her happy arms
desiccated
upon her chest,
and put her nose
outside to re-
cord the world of
whole spectacle.

She drank by small
mouthsful a grog
with two pieces of
sugar, glass, a
spoon and some rum
without making
any noise to
disturb her sleep.

And their reading
began again:
the Newspaper
of the Middle-
class Parisian –
these famished wolves
depopulate
the villages.

The cursèd war
which was never
funny, the time
of the famine
and History,
felt mortal in
its book of shells
and bottled time.

With their legs the
people's bodies
were one with the
fields; because one
dead thought arrives
to leave the men
in despair that
it would improve.

IVH 59 (coda)

Only three years
ago, there were still
heaps of people
who not only
believed themselves
but still thought that
that would last all
the added time.

And others for
which Peace was there
forever on
ground descended
to be left in
this thick and cold
silence of an
establishment.

It lasted like
that improvement
during pages
and pages of
bored mortal lies,
the loves which thus
retain you from
little droppings.

She then exclaimed
happy surprise
by closing her
book then took her
frozen mud which
again removed
at least six weeks
of charming heat.

Then the fever
knocked its heated
shoes against the
announced marriage,
listened to your
first promise to
begin against
my answered faith.

They're my lovers
known in middle-
class terms as the
small visitors –
all deserved con-
gratulations –
this did occur
from time to time.

You thus became,
during all this
time to reflect,
M. Rousseau's
young lady, dear
friend, timidly
modest adding
Jupiter's thigh.

Surely without
the penny is
a coarse word made
while laughing with
suspicion. You
astonish me!
But do your share
and judge them all.

IVH 60 (coda)

I turn over
my face, because
here the second
news is allowed
to believe me.
My rather long
convalescence
is now finished.

Ah, my god, which
war, which war, all
my thoughts, all
my wishes, must
accompany
creditable
lamentable
astonishment.

Snow continued
to choir, working
in born heavy
packages which
plugged the eyes of
a taken life
that became a
heavier pain.

If it does not
fall as snow in
winter, when thus
will it fall there?
It is truly
better falling
there in winter
than in summer.

It is, if made,
that which should be:
a family.
The main thing, but
extraordin-
arily of
nature's pure will
which never speaks.

Slipping on the
parquet floor a
volume divides
into two grogs
of quivering
water. Both will
appreciate
its bitterness.

Becoming wise
will not prevent
me from crying
large tears starting
again to plug
my frozen eyes
precisely and
atrociously.

Do you not find
It is better
still that it snows
when one is old
than one is young?
I will bid my
farewell to your
silent finish.

IVH
(special ed.)

Ornamental
education
illuminates
astonishment
realizing
aggravated
regimental
philosophies

Excavated
excessively
decorated
discoveries
accumulate
population
initially
monotonous

Interesting
anticlerics'
geranium
ceremonies
tolerated
exceptional
pessimistic
acknowledgment

Meridian
artillery
barometer
abominates
counterpart
operation's
elemental
deprivation

Reignited
virility
ruminated
idiotic
pleonasm
estimating
municipal
relationships

Continuing
historical
germanophile
newspaperman
re-examined
documented
consternation
courageously

Differently
nationalized
photographic
publications
interpreted
assiduous
methodical
predilections

Solitary
intentional
contortionist
considering
conversation
situation
agitation
infinitum

IVH (special ed. 2)

for MB

Enormously
remarkable
uncertainty
disappointed
insufficient
habitual
psychology
indifference

Reluctantly
androgynous
Canadians
exaggerate
accountable
installation's
inflexible
reality

Unexamined
necessary
Neurasthenic
respectfully
imperial
projectionist
methodically
delirious

Additional
hostilities
accompanied
military
intelligence
embraceable
retrospective
disfigurement

Quotidian
disenchantment
authorizing
periodic
spiritual
inspiration
consequently
alcoholic

Comprehensive
orchestration
naturally
penetrated
Impressionist
approbation
scandalously
victorious

Legitimate
combustible
Italian
barbarians
coagulate
instrumental
population
decoration

Monotonous
advertising
evaporates
demolishing
uniformly
necessary
intuitive
intensity

Source Text:
Raymond Queneau's *Un Rude Hiver*
Gallimard, 1946

COLOPHON

Manufactured as the first edition of ivH in the fall of 2012 by BookThug.
Distributed in Canada by the Literary Press Group: www.lpg.ca
Distributed in the USA by Small Press Distribution: www.spdbooks.org
Shop online at www.bookthug.ca

BOOK
PRODUCTION
WAR ECONOMY
STANDARD

Book Design by Michael Boughn & Victor Coleman.